和平

السلام

DAMAI

دامي

शांति

שלום

สันติภาพ

PEACE book

www.ingramcontent.com/pod-product-compliance
Lightning Source LLC
Chambersburg PA
CBHW031051250726
48655CB00004B/1395